English Face to Face

Pairwork communication activities for lower
intermediate level and beyond

David Peaty

CASSELL

Cassell Publishers Limited
Villiers House
41–47 Strand
London WC2N 5JE

The Publishers are grateful to the following for permission to
reproduce photographs:

Barnaby's Picture Library, pages 36 and 66
BBC Hulton Picture Library, pages 20 and 56
Lotus Cars, pages 30 and 68
P & O Liners, page 13

First published 1986
Reprinted 1989, 1990

ISBN 0 304 313033

Design by Barrie Richardson
Illustrations by Barrie Richardson and Martin Shovel

Set by Central Southern Typesetters, Eastbourne
Printed in Great Britain by The Bath Press, Avon

Introduction

This book contains outlines for almost 60 independent communication activities and games to be performed by pairs of students working together. Most of these activities have separate A and B roles with different instructions and information. In order to solve problems together, exchange information or achieve certain goals, students have to communicate effectively with each other. Some of the outlines have identical A and B roles and are intended to stimulate conversation and discussion. You will find the A and B roles for each activity at opposite ends of this book.

A wide variety of topics and formats has been used in order to maintain interest and to provide intensive practice with target functions and structures. Students performing activities of this kind tend to concentrate on effective communication rather than on linguistic perfection and thus express themselves more positively and without fear of making mistakes.

Suggestions to teachers

1   Pairing

How students are paired up will depend on the characteristics of the class. If you allow them to choose their own partners, they will tend to stay with the same partner throughout the course, with the result that some will work better and others will become careless. If you pair them up according to ability, you must decide which need partners of equal ability and which would benefit from having a partner of higher or lower ability.

If there is an odd number of students, one may be asked to act as your assistant, monitoring activities and making notes of problems, checking to make sure that students do not cheat by using their native language or by looking at their partner's text, and so on. Many activities may easily be adapted to include a third role; others present an opportunity for a third person to report on the information gathered or conclusion reached. If one pair finishes early, an odd student may pair up with one of the early finishers. All activities in which A and B roles are the same can be done in groups instead of pairs, e.g. 7, 10, 12 etc.

2   Language preview

Before starting each activity, you may need to review the language required. A few useful sentences and phrases are provided under the heading 'Useful language' and you may wish to add to these. On the other hand, your students may be able to communicate effectively using the English they already know and should not be forced to use certain specific expressions. In some cases, necessary structures may need reviewing or certain vocabulary may have to be presented.

3   Instructions and preliminary work

The instructions provided may not be understood first time by every student. It may therefore be helpful to explain orally what to do and how to do it. In many cases a trial run, in which pairs of students perform parts of the activity and are corrected, will be very helpful. In other cases, specific questions or responses should be elicited from random students (according to the roles they will be performing).

4 Rules

Before starting each activity, you should repeat these rules:

i) Don't look at your partner's book until you've finished.

ii) Don't let your partner see your book until you've finished.

iii) Look at your partner's face when speaking and listening.

iv) Use only English.

v) Concentrate on communicating. Don't worry about making mistakes.

vi) Don't listen to other pairs until you and your partner have finished.

5 Activities

While the students are performing activities simultaneously in pairs, you can circulate unobtrusively among them, helping when necessary and making notes of errors to be corrected later. You may also wish to evaluate individual students on their performance by taking notes or recording their conversation.

Students who finish early may be asked to monitor other pairs who are having difficulty or to make notes of their own problems.

6 Follow-up

Some activities take less time than others and may be followed by related discussion. You may wish to set aside a little time for error correction at the end of each lesson.

7 Matching activities

Many of the activities are followed by similar ones in which the roles are reversed.

E.g.
5 — A asks for information and B gives it.
6 — B asks for information and A gives it.
Likewise with activities 14 and 16, 17 and 18, 23 and 24, 27 and 28, 32 and 33, 36 and 37, 47 and 48, 51 and 52, 53 and 54.

In such activities, students should keep the same roles, i.e. A students should perform the A role in both activities.

8 Overhearing

Pairs of students should be isolated as much as possible but if overhearing becomes a problem you may wish to play background music. Alternatively, 'buffer' students could be assigned different tasks e.g. reading aloud dialogues or short plays, preparing skits, etc. A language laboratory can provide optimum audio conditions but in a very unnatural environment.

9 Repetition and stalling

Before starting the first activity and occasionally afterwards, you may need to practise the following techniques.

Asking for repetition:

Sorry?

Pardon?

Sorry, I didn't $\frac{catch}{follow}$ that.

Sorry, could you $\frac{repeat\ that?}{say\ that\ again?}$

Delaying responses:

Umm . . . Err . . .

Let me $\frac{think.}{see.}$

How $\frac{can}{shall}$ I put it?

My telephone number? Its . . .

(repeating key words)

10 Preparing your own materials

i) Information gaps can be created from any materials including those already being used on the course by means of cloze. Using typewriter correction fluid, blot out specific words to provide practice with target question forms or structures. Give A students the clozed version and B students the original. Alternatively different items can be clozed on each sheet. In either case, the answers will appear on the page in the same sequence as the questions are asked. This may be avoided by rewriting the text as is done in activities 23 and 24 of this book.

ii) Parallel texts also provide useful practice (see activity 19). Take or write two texts with similar details about different subjects in different sequence and have students find out as much as possible about their partner's subject. Here too, specific question forms or structures may be targeted.

iii) Pictures — especially spot the difference cartoons — are ideal for practising description. Photographs showing the same scene at different times are also useful e.g. a beach at noon and 6 p.m., Times Square in 1920 and 1985, etc. You can also prepare activities in which students are required to find out which person is in both pictures, as in activity 15 of this book. Photographing a friend in two different shops or at two different stations is one way of doing this.

iv) Interviews and opinion polls may be based on various formats: find out the following information about your partner (age, etc.) fill out this questionnaire by asking your partner questions, ask your partner these questions, etc.

v) Role plays, though seldom realistic communication, are useful for practising specific functions, e.g. salesman — potential customer (persuasion, negotiation, etc.). However, it is wise to avoid roles which are too specific (e.g. you are a half-deaf English landlady with three beautiful daughters) or impossible for the student to identify with. It is also prudent to consider whether the student would be able to perform the activity in his/her native language (e.g. complex business negotiations or political debates).

vi) Jumbled stories (e.g. activity 46), cartoons out of sequence (e.g. activity 12), and half-completed crossword puzzles without clues (e.g. activity 22) can also be prepared easily.

Preparing your own materials may seem troublesome, but once made, they can be used over and over again. You can also get your students to help you by contributing texts which they have clozed themselves, cartoons they have cut out, interviews they have written and so on, thus ensuring that the content interests them.

Contents

1 All about you

1 Choose a partner and introduce yourself.
Try to get the following information about your partner in a polite or friendly way. Try to remember the information.

Begin like this: Hello. My name's . . .   Hi. My Name's . . .

End like this: Well I've enjoyed talking with you.
I've enjoyed it too. Let's talk again later.

NAME

FROM

NOW LIVING IN

JOB OR STUDY

MARRIED?

CHILDREN?

HOBBIES

EVER TRAVELLED ABROAD?

IF SO, WHERE?

TAKING THIS ENGLISH COURSE BECAUSE

---

2 When you have finished, write down what you have found out.

3 Now introduce yourself to someone else and have a similar conversation.

4 Try to get to know as many people as you can before your teacher tells you to stop.

Tips

It's better to give information about yourself first,

e.g. I'm from . . . How about you?

It's better at first to ask yes/no questions, e.g. Do you live near here? rather than Wh . . . questions.

Useful language

Do you . . .?	If you don't mind my asking . . .?
Are you . . .?	Oh, that's interesting.
I suppose you . . .?	Do you? So do I.

2 How Alfred became King

Don't look at your partner's book.

1   You have part of the family tree showing the Kings and Queens of Norland. Complete this family tree by asking your partner questions.

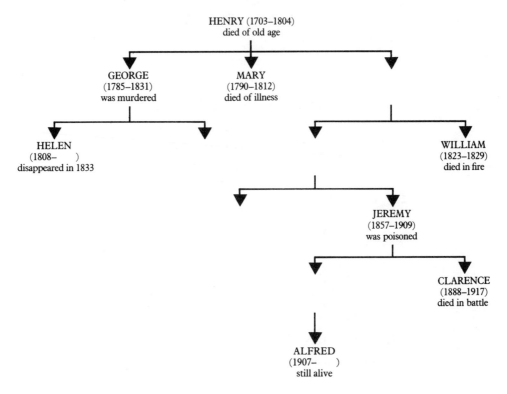

HENRY (1703–1804)
died of old age

GEORGE
(1785–1831)
was murdered

MARY
(1790–1812)
died of illness

HELEN
(1808–   )
disappeared in 1833

WILLIAM
(1823–1829)
died in fire

JEREMY
(1857–1909)
was poisoned

CLARENCE
(1888–1917)
died in battle

ALFRED
(1907–   )
still alive

Useful language

What was the name of . . .'s first child?   How did . . . die?
How do you spell that?   Pardon?
When was . . . born?   Sorry?
When did . . . die?   Could you say that again please?

2   Now try to work out with your partner the probable line of succession. Explain who succeeded whom and why.

Line of succession

name	reigned from	to
Henry	1746	1804

Useful language

Who do you think succeeded . . .?
Why?
I think so too.
I disagree. I think . . . because . . .

3   Decide what will happen when Alfred dies. (He has no children.)

3 Can you tell me the way?

Don't look at your partner's book.

1 Your partner will ask you for directions to places shown on your map. Tell him/her the way to each place, mentioning any important landmarks.

2 Then find out from your partner the way to

a) the castle   b) the campsite

Mark these on your map. Also mark any useful landmarks.

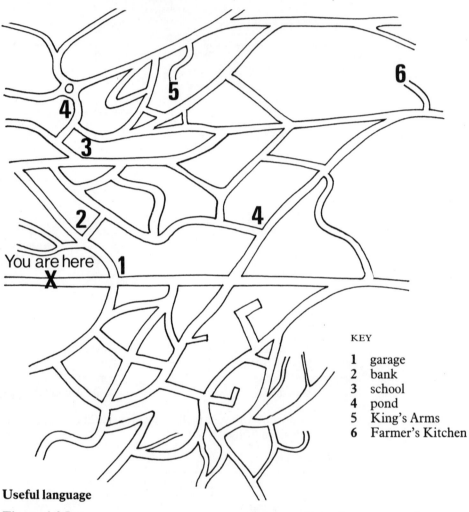

You are here
X

KEY

1 garage
2 bank
3 school
4 pond
5 King's Arms
6 Farmer's Kitchen

Useful language

The castle? Let me see.
Go straight along this road.
Turn left at the . . .
Turn right by the . . .
Take the next left.
Keep going until you come to a . . .
You'll see a . . . on your left.
The . . . is on the right.
Okay? Right?
Have you got that?

Can you tell me the way to . . .?
Sorry, could you say that again?
Pardon?
I see. May I repeat that?
  First, I . . .
  Then I . . .
Thanks a lot.

4 On the underground railway

Don't look at your partner's book.

1   You are at Southdown. Find out from your partner how to get to

    a) Cromley   **b)** Wimble   **c)** Northdown   **d)** Brewchurch

2   Your partner will ask you how to get to places shown on your map. Tell him/her how to
    get to each place.

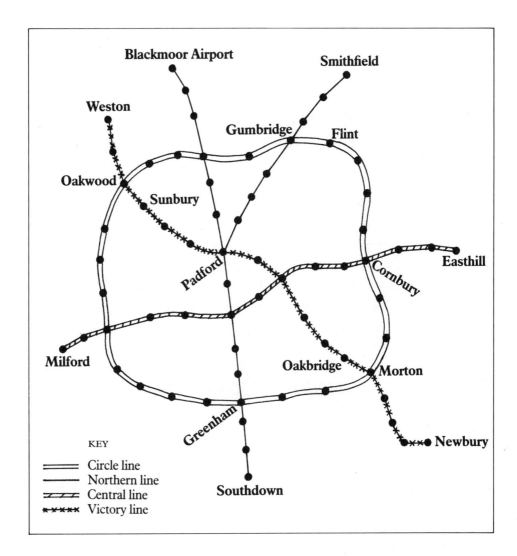

Useful language

Let me see.
Take the . . . line and get off at the . . .th station.
Change to the . . . line for . . .
. . . is the . . .th stop.
Can you tell me how to get to . . . please?
Sorry, I don't know.

5 Discount flights

Don't look at your partner's book.

1 You're a travel agent. Answer your customer's questions. Begin like this: May I help you?

destination	ATHENS	BOMBAY	MOSCOW
one way fare (£)	120	200	140
carrier	B.A.	A.I.	S.U.
flight no.	BA 123	AI 624	SU 34
departure days	1, 3, 5	2, 4	6
time of departure	09:40	10:15	10:45
arrival time (local)	10:15	00:45	18:15
duration of flight	3hrs	14hrs	5hrs
stopovers	—	Rome	—

carriers: BA – British Airways   AI – Air India   SU – Aeroflot

days: 1 – Monday   2 – Tuesday etc.

2 Your customer wants to buy a ticket.
Complete the passenger information sheet by asking questions.

Begin like this: May I have your name please?

End like this: Thank you sir/madam. Here's your ticket. Have a pleasant journey.

PASSENGER INFORMATION

Name	....
Address	....
Tel. No.	....
Destination	....
Flight No.	....
Dep. date	....
seat	smoking/no smoking
fare	1st class/economy
payment	cash/cheque/credit card

6 Mediterranean cruise

Don't look at your partner's book.

1   You want to travel by ship from Venice (Italy) to Rodos (Greece). Your partner is a travel agent. Find out:

About the service

frequency
day of departure
day of arrival
time of departure
time of arrival
ports visited en route
sightseeing time available
one way fare

About the ship

name
size
facilities available on board

2   You want to buy a ticket and make a reservation. Tell the travel agent and answer his/her questions.

7 A new restaurant

You and your partner are going to open a new restaurant.
Here are some things you need to decide:

the kind of food you will serve
the menu and prices (food and drink)
the decor
the capacity (number and size of tables)
any music?
any restrictions on smoking?
opening hours

the number of employees
employees' wages
how to hire staff
how to attract customers
how to finance your plan
the name of the restaurant

Useful language

Let's . . .
Shall we . . .?
Why don't we . . .?
Wouldn't it be a good idea to . . .?
I'd like to . . .

That's a $\left[\begin{array}{l}\text{great}\\\text{wonderful}\end{array}\right]$ idea.

I'm afraid I don't like the idea.
Okay.
I'd rather . . .
I'd prefer to . . .
All right.

8 Tell me about it

Don't look at your partner's book.

1 Find out if your partner has ever:

had an accident	got drunk	done a part-time job
been skiing	stayed in a hotel	made an international
got lost	travelled by ship	phone call
kept a pet	been to a wedding	

Begin like this: Have you ever . . .? Tell me about it.

Your partner may not be telling the truth. Look at his/her face carefully. Ask a lot of questions in order to decide whether or not his/her stories are true.

Next to the experiences listed above, write T (true) for the stories you believe, F (false) for the ones you disbelieve and ? for the ones you aren't sure about.

2 Your partner will ask you about your experiences too. When he/she asks 'Have you ever . . .' answer 'yes' each time. Talk truthfully about your real experiences. Use your imagination to talk about other experiences.

Try to make your partner think

a) that your true stories are false
b) that your fictitious stories are true.

Useful language

I don't remember exactly but . . .
I forget the exact details but . . .
An accident? Let me see. Oh yes . . .
Did you believe what I said?

9 Relatives

Find out as much as you can about each of your partner's family members and relatives. Make brief notes like this:

NAME	JOB
RELATIONSHIP	HOBBIES
AGE	INTERESTING FEATURES
ADDRESS	FEELINGS TOWARDS HIM/HER

Make sure you find out a lot about every relative, e.g. grandparents, cousins, aunts and uncles, nephews, etc.

Useful language

Have you got any . . .?
What are their names?
How do you spell that?
Tell me about . . .

Has . . . got any interesting
  features?
What's he/she like?
How do you feel towards him/her?

10 Appointments

You will be completely free next week – no work or study.

1   Choose a partner and make arrangements to do something different in the morning, afternoon or evening of each of the seven days.

     Write your seven arrangements on the schedule.

     e.g. Monday morning, tennis with Tony
         Tuesday evening, concert with Tony, etc.

2   Choose another partner. Try to fill seven more spaces in your schedule.

3   Now try to find other students who are free when you are and fill all the remaining spaces.

SCHEDULE

	morning	afternoon	evening
Monday	_____	_____	_____
Tuesday	_____	_____	_____
Wednesday	_____	_____	_____
Thursday	_____	_____	_____
Friday	_____	_____	_____
Saturday	_____	_____	_____
Sunday	_____	_____	_____

Useful language

Would you like to . . . with me some time? — I'd love to. When?
How about . . .? — That'd be fine.
Are you free on . . .? — No, I'm afraid not. How about . . .?

11 Survey 1

Don't look at your partner's book.

1   Your partner is conducting a survey. Answer his/her questions helpfully.

2   You are conducting a survey too. Interview your partner to complete the following questionnaire.

Begin like this: Excuse me. I'm doing a survey on parties. Do you mind if I ask you some questions?

End like this: Thanks a lot for your co-operation.

Parties survey

Name of respondent:

The respondent often/seldom goes to parties.

He/She prefers noisy/quiet parties at his/her own home. / at someone else's home. / pubs, restaurants, etc.

He/She likes big formal / small informal parties.

He/She usually drinks . . . at parties. He/She often/seldom/never drinks too much.

He/She prefers to talk to old/middle aged/young men/women because . . .

He/She usually talks about . . . , . . . and so on.

He/She is better at talking/listening than listening/talking.

He/She talks to strangers eagerly/reluctantly because . . .

When he/she goes to parties, he/she likes to dress up. / dress casually.

He/She spends more than/less than 15 minutes getting ready.

He/She often/seldom/never dances at parties.

The last time he/she went to a party was . . . It was a formal/informal party.

He enjoyed / She didn't enjoy it because . . .

12 Cartoon sequence

Don't look at your partner's book.

You each have three pictures from a cartoon sequence consisting of six pictures.

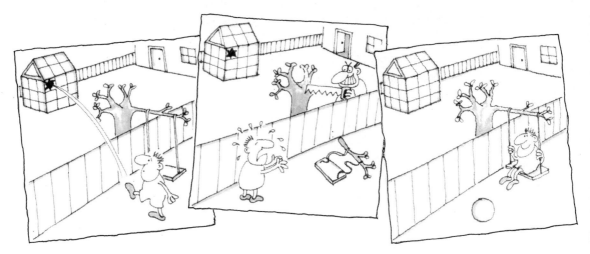

1   Describe your pictures to each other and try to work out the correct sequence of events.

2   Tell the complete story to your partner.

13 Interview

Don't look at your partner's book.

1   Ask your partner these questions.
    Discuss each answer in detail and try to remember it.

    What makes you sad?
    What are your ambitions?
    What's your favourite place?
    What's the most serious illness you've ever suffered?
    How do you spend your free time?
    What's your favourite food?
    What makes you very angry?
    If you could be anyone in the world, who would you most like to be? Why?

    Now try to jot down your partner's answers in brief.
    If you can't remember, ask again like this:

    Sorry, what did you say . . .?

2   Your partner will ask you some questions too.
    Answer each question in detail.
    When your partner seems satisfied with the answer, ask the same question yourself, like this:

    How about you? What's your . . .?

14 Identification

Don't look at your partner's book.

You are the manager of a bank which has been robbed. A witness is going to describe six people who he/she saw at the scene of the crime. Some of them are your employees, whose photographs are shown below. The others must be the robbers, since the witness was the only customer at the time. Listen carefully and identify your employees and the robbers from their descriptions. Try to imagine what the robbers look like. When you have finished, look at your partner's book and find out if your image of the robbers' appearance was good.

15 Predicament

Don't look at your partner's book.

You and your partner are driving across a big desert when your jeep breaks down. The nearest town is 200 kilometres back. You each have enough water for three days. What are you going to do?

1   These hints should give you some ideas.

You know a bit about repairing engines.
There is water in the jeep's radiator.
There is often water under the sand.
You have walked 200 kilometres many
   times before.
You don't mind walking alone.

Suggest these ideas to your partner.

Your partner also has some suggestions.
Reject them for the following reasons.

Nobody knows where you are.
There is a train strike this week.
Planes don't fly over this area.
You have no flashlight.
This route is seldom used.

2   Make more suggestions and try to find a solution to your predicament.

Useful language

Let's . . .
Why don't we . . .?
How about . . .?
We could . . .
I think we should . . .

We can't do that. (give reason)
That's no good. (give reason)
That's impossible. (give reason)
I don't think that'd be a good idea.
That's not a bad idea. Let's try it.

16 Date

You promised to meet a friend at a certain restaurant this evening. Unfortunately you have to work overtime and will be at least an hour late. To make matters worse, you don't know your friend's telephone number and cannot contact him/her.

Explain this problem to your partner and ask him/her to go to the restaurant at the appointed time and talk with your friend until you arrive.

You will have to describe the friend very carefully as there may be many people in the restaurant. You will also have to explain exactly how to get to the restaurant.

Tell your partner about your friend's interests and hobbies so he/she will know what to talk about.

17 Changing a wheel

Don't look at your partner's book.

Your partner has a problem.
Tell him/her exactly what to do.
These pictures will help you.

Useful language

		Key words	
First you . . .	Okay?	handbrake	wheel nuts
Next you . . .	Right?	hub cap	spanner
Then . . .	Are you with me?	screwdriver	jack
After that . . .	Did you follow that?		
Finally . . .	Shall I say that again?		

18 Making cookies

Don't look at your partner's book.

Your partner is going to explain how to make cookies. Listen carefully and interrupt if you don't understand. When you think you understand, try to repeat the instructions.

Useful language

(I beg your) pardon?
Sorry to interrupt but did you say . . .?

Sorry, could you say that again?
I see. Let me repeat that. First, I . . .

19 Dali and Wagner

Don't look at your partner's book.

1　Read the following information about Salvador Dali.

Salvador Dali is a famous painter. He was born in Spain in 1904. He studied painting in Madrid but was expelled from college when he was 21. He earned a living as a painter. His first great work was a surrealistic painting entitled 'The Persistence Of Memory'. In 1934 he went to the USA with his friend Helen. Their expenses were paid by Picasso.

2　Your partner has similar information about Richard Wagner. Get this information from your partner by asking questions. Write brief notes if you wish but try to remember what your partner tells you. When you have found out all you can, try to repeat it all.

3　Now your partner will ask you questions about Dali. Answer each question without giving any further information. You may prompt questions like this: You haven't asked me about . . .

When your partner has finished, he/she will try to repeat the information. Correct any errors like this: No, actually . . .

20 Conversations

Don't look at your partner's book.

1　Get your partner to tell you all about:

his/her home
a recent trip
his/her happiest memory
a recent surprise

someone he/she met for the first time recently
something he/she is looking forward to
the last movie he/she saw
something he/she intends to buy soon.

Find out as much as you can about each topic and try to keep your partner talking. When you have finished, write brief notes about your partner's answers.

Useful language

Tell me about . . .
I'd like to hear all about . . .
I'd like to know a bit more about . . .

2　Your partner will ask you to talk about certain topics too. Be talkative.

21 Television Survey

Don't look at your partner's book.

1   You are conducting a survey. Interview your partner to complete this questionnaire.

Begin like this: Excuse me. I'm conducting a survey on television. May I ask you some questions?
End like this: Well that's all. Thanks a lot for your co-operation.

viewing frequency:	every day ☐	3–6 days per week ☐	less than 3 days per week ☐

viewing time:	morning ☐	afternoon ☐	evening ☐	late night ☐

daily viewing hours:	on weekdays ☐	on Saturdays ☐	on Sundays ☐

favourite programmes	like	dislike	indifferent
drama	☐	☐	☐
comedy	☐	☐	☐
sport	☐	☐	☐
music	☐	☐	☐
quiz shows	☐	☐	☐
chat shows	☐	☐	☐
cartoons	☐	☐	☐
news	☐	☐	☐
documentaries	☐	☐	☐

reasons for watching TV:	information ☐	entertainment ☐	other

opinions:

TV programmes should be paid for by taxpayers/sponsors/viewers
reasons:

TV's effect on children is good ☐   bad ☐   insignificant ☐
reasons:

Violence and pornography should ☐ / should not ☐ be cut
reasons:

further comments:

2   Your partner is conducting a survey too. Answer his/her questions helpfully.

22 Crossword puzzle 1

Don't look at your partner's book.

You and your partner each have some of the answers to a crossword puzzle. You have no clues, however. Try to complete the puzzle by asking each other for clues, not words e.g. What's seven across? It means . . . What's three down? It's . . .

You may use a bilingual dictionary to check the meaning of a word shown on your part of the crossword puzzle but don't look for definitions in a dictionary.

Don't tell your partner any of the words he/she needs, only clues.

Don't ask for confirmation of your guesses until you have completed the puzzle.

Useful language

Can you give me another clue?
Can you tell me your clue for seven across again?
Shall I give you another clue?

23 The Statue of Liberty

Don't look at your partner's book.

Do you know this building?
What do you know about it?
Find out more from your partner and
fill in the blanks in the following article.

As your ship enters _____ Harbour, you will see a tall statue standing on a

small island named _____ . This famous statue, which is _____ feet high and

weighs _____ tons, was designed by _____ , who wanted to show his

admiration for _____ . He was inspired by the sight of a _____ during

a revolution in Paris in 18____ . He later met _____ in a

_____ and she became the model for his great work. The statue, which is made of

_____ and _____ was built in _____ and transported to New

York by _____ . It was unveiled by President _____ on October

_____th 18_____ and has since then been a symbol of freedom – hence its name, the

Statue of Liberty.

Now check your answers like this: The Statue of Liberty's in . . . , isn't it?
It stands on . . . , doesn't it? etc.

24 Himeji Castle

Don't look at your partner's book.

1 Read this article about Himeji Castle carefully.

2 Now answer your partner's questions but don't give further information.

3 Your partner will check his/her information. Answer like this:

Yes, that's correct.
No, actually . . .

Himeji Castle stands on a small hill overlooking the Inland Sea of Japan. Called the 'Egret Castle' because of its graceful appearance, it was also carefully designed from the viewpoint of defence. It originally had three moats, several metres deep, although only one now remains. The high walls are built of stone. The main keep is five storeys high and commands a fine view of the surrounding countryside. The original castle was built in 1346 but the present building dates from the year 1601. It was built by the son-in-law of the shogun Tokugawa Ieyasu and took eight years to construct.

25 Spot the differences

Don't look at your partner's book.

Describe this picture in detail and answer your partner's questions. He/she will try to find at least ten differences between your picture and his/hers.

26 Idioms, proverbs and quotes

Try to work out with your partner what the following idioms, proverbs and quotes mean. You may look up individual words in a dictionary but try to explain your interpretations using words you already know. When you and your partner have agreed on a definition, write it down.

1 Idioms

a) take for a ride

E.g. He said, 'Look at these silver spoons I bought for only five pounds'. I examined them and said, 'I'm afraid you've been taken for a ride. They're made of stainless steel, not silver'.

b) the tip of the iceberg

E.g. The police have caught a few children using dangerous drugs. I'm afraid this is just the tip of the iceberg.

c) kill two birds with one stone
E.g. Our old house was too small and too far from the station so we decided to kill two birds with one stone and buy a bigger house near the station.

2 Proverbs

a) Make hay while the sun shines.

b) Don't count your chickens before they're hatched.

c) No news is good news.

3 Quotes

a) To impatient drivers – 'It's better to arrive later in this world than early in the next.'

b) 'Death is the great equaliser.'

c) Confucius – 'Better a diamond with a flaw than a pebble without one.'

Useful language

What do you think . . . means?

I $\frac{\text{guess}}{\text{suppose}}$ it means . . .

It $\frac{\text{could}}{\text{might}}$ mean . . .

Let me give an example.

27 Tourist information 1

You work in the tourist information office of your home town. Answer your partner's questions.

Useful language

I'm afraid I don't know.
I'm not sure but I think . . .

28 Tourist information 2

Choose a partner from another country, if possible, or another town. Pretend that you know nothing about your partner's country/town. You are going to visit that place. Find out everything you need to know about:

the climate	the languages spoken
the major cities	public transport
holidays and festivals	typical souvenirs
hotels and restaurants	tipping
the best places to visit	prices and fares
culture, religion, etc.	what to wear
the money (bank notes and coins)	

Ask for useful advice

Begin like this: I'm planning to go to . . . for a few weeks. Can you tell me a bit about it?

29 Discussion

Can you think of any good ways to:

get rich quickly?	protect your home from thieves?
learn to speak English fluently?	spend 10 dollars?
live to the age of 100?	spend 10 thousand dollars?
find your future husband or wife?	become famous?
cut the number of traffic accidents?	spend your life after retirement?

Discuss each question with your partner and try to choose the best answer.

Useful language

One way to . . . is to . . .	I agree.
A better way is to . . .	I disagree.
What do you think?	In my opinion, the best way is . . .

30 Resort island

You and your partner have bought a small island and want to develop it as a tourist resort in order to attract a lot of visitors. On the next page is your publicity brochure.

Discuss the details with your partner and then fill in the blanks together.

Next, discuss the best location for the amenities you have chosen (hotels, restaurants, sports facilities, etc.) and mark these on your map. Decide how much to charge for transport, entertainment, etc.

Finally, discuss how to publicise your resort and attract visitors in all seasons.

Useful language

What shall we . . .?	That's a great idea.
Why don't we . . .?	I don't think that'd be a good idea.
How about . . .?	I'd rather . . .
Let's . . .	I think I'd prefer to . . .
I think we should . . .	Okay.

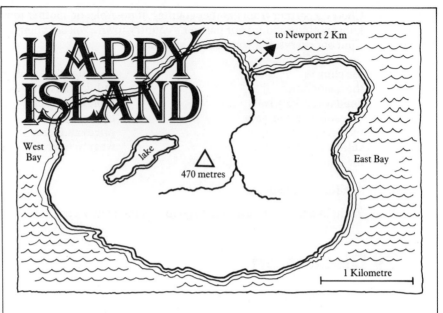

Come to Happy Island. There's fun for everybody!

For children, there's _____ and _____ .

For adults, we have _____ , _____ and _____ .

Do you like sports? You can _____ , _____ and _____ in summer.

You can _____ in winter; and you can _____ all year round.

We have accommodation to suit every budget. Stay in _____ ,

_____ or _____ .

Our restaurants cater for all tastes. Eat _____ at the

or _____ at the _____ .

You'll love travelling by _____ or _____ around the island.

(Sorry, no cars!)

Why not book your Happy Island holiday now?

Newport to Happy Island by _____ takes _____ minutes

and costs _____ .

Admission fee is _____ .

31 Treasure Island

Don't look at your partner's book.

You and your partner are going to look for treasure on an island. You each have a map with a different part of the route marked on it.

a) Draw on your map the part of the route explained by your partner.

b) Explain to your partner the part of the route shown on your map, giving suitable warnings of danger as shown by the symbols which are explained in the key.

c) Discuss the best way to cross each river and the best route from the first bridge to the second.

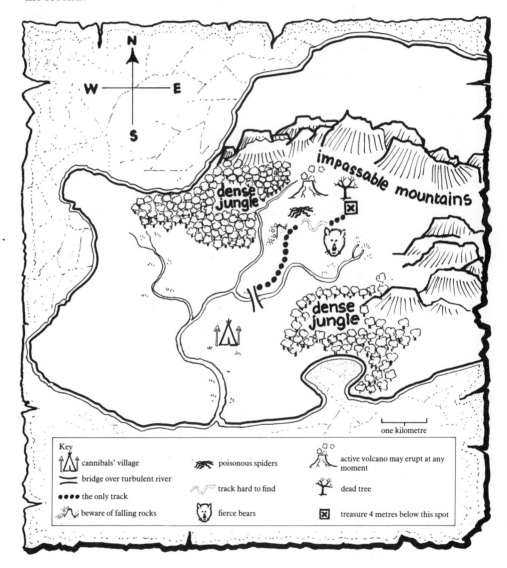

one kilometre

Key

🏕️ cannibals' village   🕷️ poisonous spiders   🌋 active volcano may erupt at any moment

〰️ bridge over turbulent river   〰️ track hard to find   🌳 dead tree

●●●● the only track   🪨 beware of falling rocks   🐻 fierce bears   ☒ treasure 4 metres below this spot

Useful language

Go west for about 2 kilometres
We'll have to watch out for . . .
We must be careful not to . . .

27

32 The Grand Hotel

Don't look at your partner's book.

1   Read the following information carefully.

The Grand Hotel, OSBORNE

The Grand is a modern four-storey hotel located on a small hill overlooking Osborne Bay, only ten minutes walk from the beach and fifteen minutes bus ride from Osborne Station. It has 120 rooms, 40 of which have private baths or showers. Each room is centrally-heated in winter and some rooms have colour televisions and telephones. Amenities include a superb restaurant, two bars, a swimming pool, a television lounge and a sports room. Golf, tennis, horseriding and sailing facilities are within easy walking distance.

Room charges per night:

single with bath/shower	28 dollars
single without bath/shower	22 dollars
double with bath	40 dollars
twin with shower	44 dollars

---

2   You work for the Grand Hotel as a reservations clerk. You are answering a telephone inquiry.

Answer each question. If the caller wants to make a reservation, fill out the booking form below.

BOOKING FORM

name(s)	
address & tel. no.	
type of room required	
dates of stay	
meals if needed	

Begin like this: Good morning/afternoon. Grand Hotel. May I help you?

Useful language

May I ask . . .?
Could you tell me . . .?

33 Homestay programme

Don't look at your partner's book.

English Homestay and Study Programme
Tel. 90642 for details.

You are planning to stay with an English family and study English at a language school for 2 months. Telephone the number advertised to find out:

Homestay	School
cost	cost
includes meals?	hours per week and length of course
type of family	size of classes
sharing room?	type of English taught
location	any exams?
own key?	social and cultural activities
	nationalities of other students
	graduation certificate?

and anything else you need to know.

Begin like this: Good morning. I'm calling about your English Homestay and Study Programme. Could you tell me . . .?

End like this: Well I think that's all. I'll think it over and let you know if I decide to go. Thank you very much. Goodbye.

34 Topics

Don't look at your partner's book.

1   Get your partner to talk for two minutes on each of these topics.

eggs   dreams   cats
    the moon   yellow

If your partner remains silent for more than ten seconds during the talk, impose a penalty of one minute extra speaking time.

Start like this: Tell me what you know about . . .

2   Your partner will ask you to talk for two minutes on certain other topics. Once you start, you must keep talking. If you remain silent for more than ten seconds during the talk, you will have to talk for an extra minute as a penalty.

If you need time to think, use the following hesitation techniques.

Useful language

Hesitation: Eggs? er . . . mmm . . . Well . . .
             Let me see.
             How shall I put it?
             and . . . also . . . so . . .

Rephrasing: I mean . . .
             What I want to say is . . .
             Let me put it another way.

35 Explanations

Don't look at your partner's book.

1 Get your partner to explain the following. Insist on a clear explanation, even if you already understand. Don't correct your partner even if you know he/she is wrong.

a) the meaning of: bank   cousin   passport   rainbow

b) the difference between 'look' and 'see'

c) the school system of your partner's country

d) how to play a certain sport (including the rules, scoring, etc.)

e) how to make a cup of tea or coffee

Useful language

Could you tell me what . . . means?

Can you explain . . .?

Pardon? Sorry? I'm afraid I don't understand.
                              don't follow you.

Would you mind explaining that again?
                                  another way?

Sorry but I still don't understand . . .

I see. You mean . . .?

2 Your partner will ask you to explain some things too. Do your best. Use your imagination if necessary. You must give an explanation but it doesn't matter if you are wrong. Do not use a dictionary. Try to explain using words you already know.

Useful language

Pardon? Sorry?

Could you spell that?

I think it means . . .
  believe

I'm not sure but I think . . .
                     suppose

I don't know exactly . . . but I think . . .
              much about   guess

36 The Lotus Excel

1 Read this information carefully.

The Lotus Excel is a four-seat sports car with a 2 litre engine. It has a top speed of 132 mph and an average consumption of 28 mpg. It can cruise approximately 420 miles with a tankful of petrol. It has a luggage capacity of 13 cu ft. The price of £7250 includes a 5-speed gearbox, power steering and air conditioning. Car stereo and alloy wheels are optional extras.

2 You are a car salesman.

A customer is interested in buying a Lotus Excel. Answer his/her questions.

Begin like this: May I help you, sir/madam?

37 House for sale

You want to buy a house. You saw one advertised in yesterday's newspaper and are calling for further information. You want to know

the location	the size	the type of heating
the price	the style	if there is a garden
the age	the colour	if there is a garage
the condition	the construction materials	

and anything else you think is important.

Begin like this: Good morning (afternoon). I believe you advertised a house for sale. Is it still available?

Make an appointment to see the house like this: When can I . . .?

Don't forget to find out the address!

38 Tall story 1

You've just seen this scene.
Tell your partner all about it.
Answer his/her questions exactly because he/she is very sceptical and might not believe you.

Begin like this: You might find this hard to believe but I've just . . .

39 Tall story 2

Don't look at your partner's book.

He/she is going to tell you about an experience he/she has just had. Be sceptical. Ask a lot of questions and try to prove that he/she is making the story up.

Useful language

You must be joking.
You can't be serious.
Do you really expect me to believe that?

A

40 Opinions 1

Discuss with your partner and decide together:

a) the most useful possession you both have

b) the best film you've both seen

c) the most unusual thing you've both seen

d) the best book you've both read

e) the worst habit you both have

f) the most interesting place you've both visited

g) the best TV programme you both watch

h) the most unpleasant experience you've both had

E.g.

A   What's your most useful possession?

B   Let me see. My bicycle, I suppose.

A   Oh. I haven't got a bicycle. I think my most useful possession is my calculator. Have you got a calculator?

B   Yes, but I don't think it's very useful. How about . . .?

Useful language

Have you got . . .?

Have you ever . . .?

I think . . .

I suppose . . .

I agree/disagree.

Surely . . . is more . . .

41 Sketches

Don't let your partner see your book.

1   Tell your partner how to draw your picture. Don't say what it is – let him/her guess.

2   Your partner will tell you how to draw his/her picture. Draw it in the space on the right of your page next to your picture. Try to guess what it is.

your picture   your partner's picture

Useful language

Draw a horizontal line from $\begin{matrix}\text{vertical} \\ \text{top left} \\ \text{bottom right} \\ \text{diagonal}\end{matrix}$ to . . .

Draw a $\begin{matrix}\text{large circle} \\ \text{small triangle} \\ \text{rectangle}\end{matrix}$ $\begin{matrix}\text{square} \\ \text{above} \\ \text{below}\end{matrix}$ · · ·

This line is $\begin{matrix}\text{half} \\ \text{twice}\end{matrix}$ as long as . . .

This line is the same length as . . .

From the $\begin{matrix}\text{middle} \\ \text{end}\end{matrix}$ of this line, . . .

Sorry but I didn't understand. Could you say that again?
I see. The vertical line goes from . . . to . . .
How long is this line? How big is the circle?

42 News

1   You have just read this morning's 'Times'.
These were the headlines:

Hotel Fire   Bank Robbery   Pensioner Wins A Million Dollars

Imagine the details.

Your partner is going to ask you questions about each report.

2   Your partner has just read a different newspaper, 'The Herald'. Find out what the main news was in that newspaper. Ask questions to get as many details as you can.

Begin like this: Anything interesting in 'The Herald' today?

43 Scandal

1   A friend of yours saw your partner behaving very strangely yesterday.

At 7 a.m. he/she was riding a donkey, dressed like Napoleon.

At 2 p.m. he/she was sitting in a litter basket with a camera.

At 6 p.m. he/she was chasing a hen, clutching a knife and fork.

These incidents happened on a local street. Demand a complete explanation from your partner and try to find out as much as possible about the surrounding circumstances and how the incidents are connected.

Useful language

A friend of mine saw you . . .ing on a local street at . . . o'clock.
Would you mind telling me what $\begin{matrix}\text{you were up to?} \\ \text{was going on?}\end{matrix}$

2   You also have been seen behaving very strangely. Explain your behaviour to your partner's satisfaction.

Useful language

Yes, I admit that it seems a strange thing to do.
You see . . .

A 44 Countries

Don't look at your partner's book.

	ECUADOR	ALBANIA	ICELAND	YOUR PARTNER'S COUNTRY
Location	S. America			
Population	9 million			
Language	Spanish			
Religion	Catholic			
Capital city	Quito			
Highest mountain	Chimborozo 6600 metres			
Biggest export	oil			
Life expectancy	63 years			
Political system	Republic			

1 Working by yourself, fill in as many spaces as you can in the chart. You have only five minutes to do this.

2 Working with a partner,
a) Confirm what you've written in the second column, e.g. Albania's in . . . , isn't it?

Find out what you don't know, e.g. Can you tell me what language they speak in . . .?

b) Answer your partner's questions about Ecuador.

c) Compare your ideas about Iceland like this:

I think . . .	So do I./Do you? I think . . .
Do you know . . .?	I'm not sure but I think . . .
	No. I'm afraid I have no idea.

d) Confirm what you have written about your partner's country and find out what you don't know.

e) Answer your partner's questions about your country.

3 Listen carefully. Your teacher will tell you all you need to know about Iceland. Fill in the spaces with the correct data. What did you find most surprising?

4 Discuss with your partner which of the countries you have just talked about you would most or least like to live in. Why?

45 Stories 1

Don't look at your partner's book.

1 Your partner has a diamond. Find out exactly how he/she got it. Ask a lot of questions to get the whole story.

2 You have a gold coin. How you got it is shown below. Tell your partner the story, making it as interesting as possible. Use your imagination to fill in the details.

46 Stories 2

Don't look at your partner's book.

Two separate stories have got mixed up. You have some sentences from each story.
Your partner has the other sentences. Work out the two complete stories with your
partner without looking at each other's sentences.

A policeman came along.

He also used a talking parrot in his act.

The bird looked at the magician with
admiration.

An old man was driving his donkey cart
along a country road.

He pulled rabbits out of a hat and made
them disappear.

'Why are you hitting that bridge with a
hammer?' he asked.

One day, the ship hit an iceberg.

'Now that was really impressive,' it
said. 'How did you do that trick?'

'Why don't you dig the ground under
the bridge instead?' asked the
policeman.

Useful language

Sorry, could you say that again?
What do you think the first sentence is?

Can you tell me your third sentence again?
I've got a sentence which comes before that.

47 Nepal

1 Read this article about
Nepal. You may use a
dictionary if you want.

Nepal is a small country located between Tibet and India. It extends 500 miles from
east to west and 100 miles from north to south and has a total area of 54,362 square
miles. It has a population of 11.3 million, most of whom are Mongol or Aryan. Nepal
is a constitutional monarchy and is ruled by King Mahendra. The main religions are
Hinduism and Buddhism. Geographically, Nepal consists of three distinct regions:
the Himalayan mountains, the Himalayan foothills and the Terai plains. The climate
is temperate in the mountains and tropical in the plains, with a maximum temperature
of 105°F and an average rainfall of 60 inches per year, most of which comes in the
rainy season from June to September. Most Nepalis are engaged in the production of
rice, their main food, or in tourism, which is the country's principal source of foreign
currency.

2 Answer your partner's questions. Don't give any additional information.

48 New Zealand

Don't look at your partner's book.

1 Think about these questions for a while.

Have you ever been to New Zealand?
If not, would you like to go? Why (not)?
What do you think the people are like? Friendly?
How about the scenery?
What do you know about New Zealand's history?
In what ways is New Zealand different from your country?

2 Fill in the blanks in the following article by asking your partner questions.

New Zealand, a small island nation located _____ miles east of Australia, has

a population of about _____ million. The native people, called _____,

are greatly outnumbered by descendants of settlers from _____, the country

from which New Zealand became independent in the year 19_____.

New Zealand consists of _____ islands with a total area of _____ square

miles. The two largest islands, _____ and _____, are separated by the

_____ Strait, which is _____ miles wide at the narrowest point. The largest

towns, _____ and _____, the capital, are located on _____

Island. New Zealand has many farms and its main exports are _____,

_____ and _____. There are also many mountains, the highest of which is

named after _____, a British _____.

49 Opinions 2

Discuss with your partner and decide together what is:

a) the most significant event of the 20th century so far

b) the greatest invention or discovery waiting to be made

c) the biggest danger facing the world today

d) the nation which has contributed most to human development

e) the most difficult aspect of English for foreign students

f) the most important quality needed by a good teacher

Useful language

As I see it, . . .
If you ask me, . . .
I suppose . . .

Really? But don't you think . . .?
Yes, that's just what I think.

50 Crossword puzzle 2

Don't look at your partner's book.

You and your partner each have some of the answers to this crossword puzzle. However, you have no clues. Try to complete the puzzle by asking each other for clues, not words.

E.g. What's 7 across? What's 1 down?

You may use a bilingual dictionary to check the meaning of a word shown on your part of the crossword puzzle but don't look for definitions in a dictionary.

Don't tell your partner any of the words he/she needs, only clues.

Don't ask for confirmation of your guesses.

Two words are missing. Try to guess these and make up appropriate clues.

51 Lock

Explain to your partner what a canal lock is and how it works, without showing the diagram.

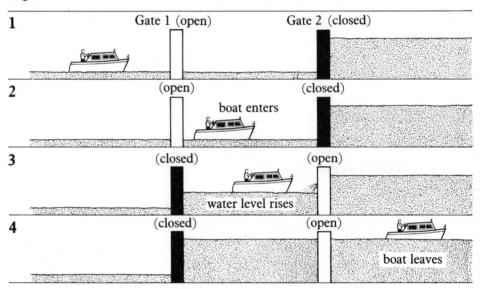

Useful language

It is used for . . .
It consists of . . .
When someone wants to take their boat upstream, . . .
downstream, . . .

Are you with me?
OK?
You see?

52 Water lift

Don't look at your partner's book.

Find out from your partner what a water lift is used for and how it works. Try to draw a diagram.

Useful language

Can you tell me . . .?   Would you explain that last part again?
Sorry but I didn't follow that.   I see.

53 Job interview 1

Your travel agency has advertised a vacancy for a homestay coordinator. Interview your first applicant and fill out this form.

Details of applicant

NAME

ADDRESS

TEL. NO.

DATE OF BIRTH

AGE

PLACE OF BIRTH

NATIONALITY

PRESENT OCCUPATION

MARITAL STATUS

DETAILS OF PREVIOUS EMPLOYMENT (JOB AND DATES)

EDUCATIONAL BACKGROUND (SECONDARY SCHOOL AND COLLEGE)

QUALIFICATIONS OBTAINED

FOREIGN LANGUAGE ABILITY

DETAILS OF OVERSEAS TRAVEL

INTERESTS AND HOBBIES

REASONS FOR APPLYING FOR THIS JOB

---

2   Then answer the applicant's questions about the job.

Here are some details about the job:

duties – coordinating homestay programmes in the U.S. for students from your country

pay – 700 dollars per month + travel expenses
hours – irregular. Must be available all day every day to deal with emergencies.

holidays – 1 week in May or November (unpaid)

pension – none

fringe benefits – free travel and accommodation (without meals) in U.S. and full insurance for medical expenses.

Begin like this: Pleased to meet you, . . . My name's . . .
                 Thank you for coming.
                 First, I'd like to ask you some questions.

End like this: Well thank you for coming, . . .
                 We'll let you know our decision within a week or so.

54 Job interview 2

You are applying for a job in London as a teacher of your native language. The school principal will interview you. Answer each question truthfully. Then try to find out this information about the job:

duties   hours   pay   holidays   fringe benefits   pension

average age of students   period of employment

Begin like this: Good morning. My name's . . .

Ask about the job like this: May I ask a few questions about the job?

End like this: It was nice meeting you. I hope to hear from you soon. Goodbye.

55 A deliberate mistake

Don't look at your partner's book.

You and your partner each have a picture.

In each picture the artist has made a deliberate mistake, e.g. something is missing or is in the wrong place.

Find out what is wrong with your partner's picture by asking questions.

Answer your partner's questions about your picture but do not help him/her to guess the mistake.

56 Contest

Work with a partner. Try to finish before the other students.

1   Work out together what these abbreviations stand for:

P T O   RIP   G M T   VIP   PhD   o n o   c/o   Ltd

Ave   Sq

2   Complete these similes. If you don't know the standard expression, use your imagination.

as weak as a *kitten*	as deaf as	to run like
as old as	as fit as	to eat like
as mad as	to sing like *a bird*	to smoke like
as thin as	to swim like	to sleep like

3   Write down:

6 words whose plural form doesn't end in s   3 occupations dealing with animals
5 things you can do with an umbrella   2 kinds of birds
4 kinds of catastrophe   1 word meaning 'cannot be anticipated'

Useful language

What do you think . . . stands for?   Let's do the easy ones first.
Perhaps it means . . .   We've finished!

57 Deductions

Don't look at your partner's book.

Try to solve this puzzle with your partner by exchanging information and deductions. Do not write down your partner's sentences. You may only write data in the space beneath each house.

There are five houses in Mill Lane. Each is a different colour and is occupied by one person. Each person has a different job and uses a different vehicle.

Work out the following details about each person:

his/her name
his/her occupation
where he/she lives

the colour of his/her house
the vehicle he/she uses

Clues

Number 1 is blue.
Mr. Harris has a motorbike.
Mr. Smith lives next door to a mechanic.
One of Mr. Clark's neighbours has a yellow house.
A banker lives in the red house.
Miss Anderson has a bicycle.
Miss Jones' neighbour has a Rolls Royce.
The owner of the green house has a Honda Civic.

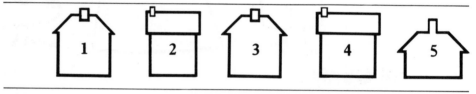

Colour					
Name					
Job					
Vehicle					

58 Impressions

Find out what your partner thought of your English course.

Talk about:

the curriculum
the teachers
the cost
the length of the course

the materials used
the other students
the classroom facilities
your partner's progress

Agree or disagree with your partner's comments and talk about your own impressions.

Useful language

What do you think of . . .?
How did you find . . .?
I thought it was quite/very . . .
I found it quite/very . . .

I thought so too.
Oh, I wouldn't say that.
Why do you think so?

B

B

1 All about you

1   Choose a partner and introduce yourself.

Try to get the following information about your partner in a polite or friendly way. Try to remember the information.

Begin like this: Hello. My name's . . .   Hi. My Name's . . .

End like this: Well I've enjoyed talking with you.
I've enjoyed it too. Let's talk again later.

NAME

FROM

NOW LIVING IN

JOB OR STUDY

MARRIED?

CHILDREN?

HOBBIES

EVER TRAVELLED ABROAD?

IF SO, WHERE?

TAKING THIS ENGLISH COURSE BECAUSE

2   When you have finished, write down what you have found out.

3   Now introduce yourself to someone else and have a similar conversation.

4   Try to get to know as many people as you can before your teacher tells you to stop.

Tips

It's better to give information about yourself first,

e.g. I'm from . . . How about you?

It's better at first to ask yes/no questions, e.g. Do you live near here? rather than Wh . . . questions.

Useful language

Do you . . .?   If you don't mind my asking, . . .?
Are you . . .?   Oh, that's interesting.
I suppose you . . .?   Do you? So do I.

2 How Alfred became King

Don't look at your partner's book.

1   You have part of the family tree showing the Kings and Queens of Norland. Complete this family tree by asking your partner questions.

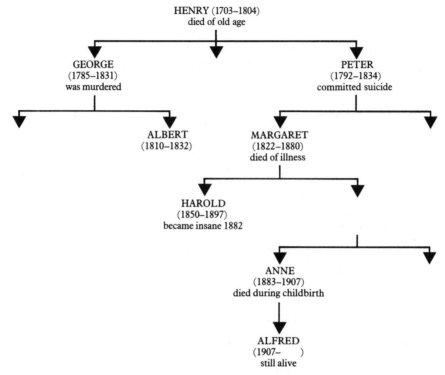

Useful language

What was the name of . . .'s first child?   How did . . . die?

How do you spell that?   Pardon?

When was . . . born?   Sorry?

When did . . . die?   Could you say that again please?

2   Now try to work out with your partner the probable line of succession. Explain who succeeded whom and why.

Line of succession

name	reigned from	to
Henry	1746	1804

Useful language

Who do you think succeeded . . .?

Why?

I think so too.

I disagree. I think . . . because . . .

3   Decide what will happen when Alfred dies. (He has no children.)

3 Can you tell me the way?

Don't look at your partner's book.

1 Find out from your partner the way to

a) the King's Arms (a pub)
b) the Farmer's Kitchen (a restaurant)

Mark these on your map. Also mark any important landmarks.

2 Your partner will ask you for directions to places shown on your map. Tell him/her the way to each place, mentioning any important landmarks.

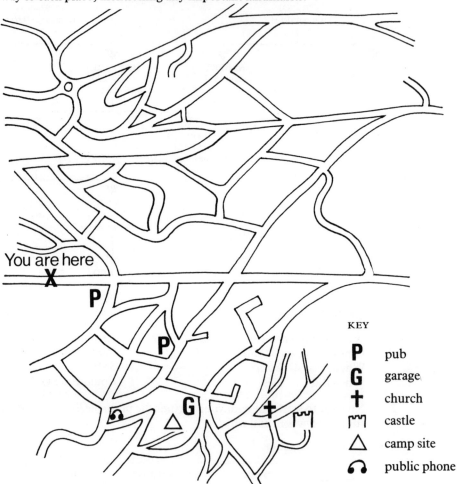

You are here
X

KEY

P	pub
G	garage
†	church
🏰	castle
△	camp site
🎧	public phone

Useful language

Can you tell me the way to . . .?
Sorry, can you say that again?
Pardon?
I see. May I repeat that?
First I . . . Then . . .
Thanks a lot.

The . . .? Let me see.
Go straight along this road.
Turn right at the . . .
Turn left by the . . . Okay?
Take the next right.
Keep going until you come to a . . .
You'll see the . . . on your left.
Have you got that?
Shall I repeat that?

4 On the underground railway

Don't look at your partner's book.

1   Your partner will ask you how to get to various places shown on your map. Tell him/her how to get to each place. You are both at Southdown now.

2   Find out from your partner how to get to

   a) Flint   **b)** Sunbury   **c)** Gumbridge   **d)** Camhurst

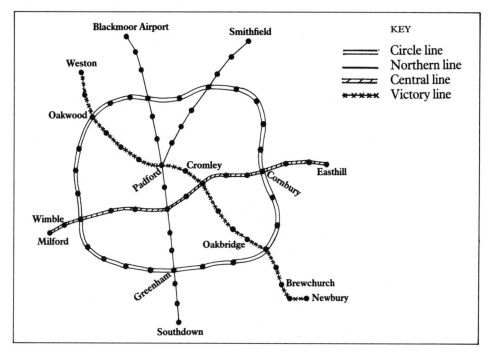

Useful language

Let me see.
Take the . . . line and get off at the . . .th station.
Change to the . . . line for . . .
. . . is the . . .th stop.
Can you tell me how to get to . . . please?
Sorry, I don't know.

5 Discount flights from London

Don't look at your partner's book.

You want to fly to Bombay soon. Your partner is a travel agent. Find out:

if there are cheap flights	how long the flight takes
the fare	days on which you can leave
if there are stopovers	departure and arrival time
the airline	flight number

anything else you need to know

Then buy a ticket and make a reservation.

6 Mediterranean cruise

Venice to Haifa on 'Stella Helena'.

Day	Port	Arr	Dep	one way fares from Venice ($US)			
				deluxe	2 berth	4 berth	deck reclining seat
Mon	Venice	08.00	10.00	deluxe	2 berth	4 berth	deck reclining seat
Tue	Corfu	07.00	07.30	400	220	150	100
Wed	Piraeus	09.00	13.00	560	300	240	180
Thu	Rodos	07.00	08.00	720	380	300	220
Fri	Haifa	09.30	14.30	800	440	340	240

About the 'Stella Helena'

Size: 2450 tons
Capacity: 80 cabins, 240 reclining seats
Facilities: restaurant, bar, pool, duty-free shop, money exchange

1   You are a travel agent. Your partner is a customer. Answer his/her questions and sell him/her a ticket.

2   Then complete the reservation form.

RESERVATION FORM

Name ....

Address ....

Tel. No. ....

Destination ....

Port of departure ....

Ship ....

Departure date ....

Class   deluxe   2 berth   4 berth   deck

Begin like this: May I help you?

7 A new restaurant

You and your partner are going to open a new restaurant.
Here are some things you need to decide:

the kind of food you will serve
the menu and prices (food and drink)
the decor
the capacity (number and size of tables)
any music?
any restrictions on smoking?
opening hours

the number of employees
employees' wages
how to hire staff
how to attract customers
how to finance your plan
the name of the restaurant

Useful language

Let's . . .
Shall we . . .?
Why don't we . . .?
Wouldn't it be a good idea to . . .?
I'd like to . . .
That's a $\begin{bmatrix} \text{great} \\ \text{wonderful} \end{bmatrix}$ idea.

I'm afraid I don't like the idea.
Okay.
I'd rather . . .
I'd prefer to . . .
All right.

8 Tell me about it

Don't look at your partner's book.

1   Your partner will ask you if you have experienced certain things.

When he/she asks 'Have you ever . . .?' answer 'yes' each time.

Talk truthfully about your real experiences.

Use your imagination to talk about other experiences.

Try to make your partner think

a) that your true stories are false
b) that your fictitious stories are true.

Useful language

Camping? Let me see. Oh yes . . .
I forget the exact details but . . .
I don't remember exactly but . . .
Did you believe what I said?

2   Now find out if your partner has ever:

been camping   had his/her fortune told
moved house   won a competition
been robbed   got engaged to be married
climbed a mountain   made a speech in front of a large
travelled by plane   audience
spoken with a famous person

Begin like this: Have you ever . . .? Tell me about it.

Your partner may not be telling the truth.

Look at his/her face carefully.

Ask a lot of questions in order to decide whether or not each story is true.

Next to the experiences listed above, write T (true) for the stories you believe, F (false) for the ones you disbelieve and ? for the ones you aren't sure about.

9   Relatives

Find out as much as you can about each of your partner's family members and relatives. Make brief notes like this:

NAME	JOB
RELATIONSHIP	HOBBIES
AGE	INTERESTING FEATURES
ADDRESS	FEELINGS TOWARDS HIM/HER

Make sure you find out a lot about every relative, e.g. grandparents, cousins, aunts and uncles, nephews, etc.

Useful language

Have you got any . . .?   Has . . . got any interesting
What are their names?   features?
How do you spell that?   What's he like?
Tell me about . . .   How do you feel towards him?

10 Appointments

You will be completely free next week – no work or study.

1   Choose a partner and make arrangements to do something different in the morning, afternoon or evening of each of the seven days.

    Write your seven arrangements on the schedule.

    e.g. Monday morning, tennis with Tony
         Tuesday evening, concert with Tony, etc.

2   Choose another partner. Try to fill seven more spaces in your schedule.

3   Now try to find other students who are free when you are and fill all the remaining spaces.

SCHEDULE

	morning	afternoon	evening
Monday	_____	_____	_____
Tuesday	_____	_____	_____
Wednesday	_____	_____	_____
Thursday	_____	_____	_____
Friday	_____	_____	_____
Saturday	_____	_____	_____
Sunday	_____	_____	_____

Useful language

Would you like to . . . with me some time?
— I'd love to. When?
How about . . .?
— That'd be fine.
Are you free on . . .?
— No, I'm afraid not. How about . . .?

B

11 Survey 1

Don't look at your partner's book.

1   You are conducting a survey. Interview your partner to complete the following questionnaire.

Begin like this: Excuse me. I'm conducting a survey on holidays. May I ask you a few questions?

End like this: I think that's all. Thanks a lot for your time.

Holidays survey

Name of respondent:

The respondent often/seldom goes away on holiday.

He/She prefers to spend his/her holidays abroad./in his/her own country.

He/She prefers to travel alone/with friends/on a package tour because . . .

His/Her favourite means of transport is . . . This is because . . .

He plans/She does not plan his/her holidays very carefully.

He/She prefers to stay in expensive hotels/cheap hotels/youth hostels or a tent because . . .

He/She always takes a lot of/little money

He usually/She seldom takes photographs because . . .

He/She prefers active/adventurous/relaxing holidays and likes to . . . on holiday.

He/She thinks the most important factors in deciding where to spend a holiday are:

He/She spent his/her last holiday . . .ing in . . ./at home.

He enjoyed/She did not enjoy it because . . .

---

2   Your partner is conducting a survey too. Answer his/her questions helpfully.

12 Cartoon sequence

Don't look at your partner's book.

You each have three pictures from a cartoon sequence consisting of six pictures.

1   Describe your pictures to each other and try to work out the correct sequence of events.

2   Tell the complete story to your partner.

13 Interview

Don't look at your partner's book.

1   Your partner is going to ask you some questions.
Answer each question in detail.
When your partner seems satisfied with the answer, ask the same question yourself, like this:

How about you? What's your . . .?

2   Now ask your partner these questions.
Discuss each answer in detail and try to remember it.

What frightens you most?
What's your most precious possession?
What type of person would you most like to marry?
What do you most dislike doing?
What job would you most like to have?
What's your favourite day of the week?
What's your biggest achievement?
What would you most like to do right now?

Now try to jot down your partner's answers in brief.
If you can't remember, ask again like this:

Sorry, I've forgotten what you said your . . . was.

B

14 Identification

Don't look at your partner's book.

You were the only customer in a bank at the time of a robbery. You saw six people, whose pictures are shown below. Some of them work for the bank, the others are robbers. Describe them all to your partner, the manager of the bank, to find out who were the employees and who were the robbers.

Useful words:

moustache	bald	curly hair
beard	clean-shaven	wavy hair

15 Predicament

Don't look at your partner's book.

You and your partner are driving across a big desert when your jeep breaks down. The nearest town is 200 kilometres back. You each have enough water for six days. What are you going to do?

1   These hints should give you some ideas.

Your friends expect to see you tomorrow.
There's a railway line about 50 kilometres east.
You can be seen from the air.
Walking at night needs less water.
Other people also like driving across deserts.

Suggest these ideas to your partner.

Your partner also has some suggestions. Reject them for the following reasons.

You forgot to bring tools.
Radiator water is too dirty to drink.
You don't have a shovel.
It would take more than four days to cover 200 kilometres.
It's dangerous to be alone in the desert.

54

2   Make more suggestions and try to find a solution to your predicament.

Useful language

Let's . . .	We can't do that. (give reason)
Why don't we . . .?	That's no good. (give reason)
How about . . .?	That's impossible. (give reason)
We could . . .	That wouldn't be a good idea.
I think we should . . .	Okay, let's do that.

16 Date

Your partner has a problem. Find out what it is.

You can help, but you need the following information:

the appointed time
directions to the appointed place (you don't know it)
an exact description of your partner's friend
(age, height, weight, hairstyle, colour of hair, other features.)

Also find out about his/her interests and hobbies so you know what to talk about.

Ask as many questions as you can to get the exact details.

17 Changing a wheel

Don't look at your partner's book.

Your car has a puncture. Ask your partner what to do. Listen to his/her instructions very carefully. If you don't understand anything, ask him/her to explain again. When your partner has finished explaining, try to repeat the instructions.

Useful language

Pardon?
Sorry?

Sorry, could you say/explain that again?

Sorry but I didn't understand./follow that.

I see. First I . . . Then . . .

Key words

handbrake
hub cap
screwdriver
wheel nut
spanner
jack

18 Making cookies

Ingredients:

half cup margarine
half cup sugar
1 egg
2 cups flour
1 cup oats
2 teaspoons coconut
2 teaspoons baking powder

Directions:

Mix the margarine and sugar in a bowl.
Beat the mixture until it becomes creamy.
Heat it until it melts.
Add the egg and beat the mixture again.
Mix the other ingredients in a large bowl.
Add the egg mixture and stir briskly with a wooden spoon.
Shape the mixture into a roll.
Cut the roll with a sharp knife into thin slices.
Lay each slice on a greased metal tray with plenty of space.
Place the tray in a preheated oven and bake for 30 minutes at 250 degrees Centigrade.

Read these instructions very carefully.
Try to remember them, and then cover them up with a piece of paper.
Tell your partner how to make cookies.
These pictures will help you. Try not to look back at the instructions.

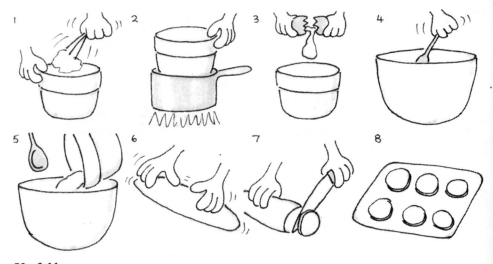

Useful language

First you . . .	After that . . .	Right?	Did you follow that?
Then . . .	Finally . . .	Are you with me?	Shall I say that again?
Next . . .	Okay?		

Key words

mix	heat	add	squeeze
beat	melt	stir	bake

19 Dali and Wagner

Don't look at your partner's book.

1   Read the following information about
Richard Wagner.

Richard Wagner was a famous
composer. He was born in Germany in
1813. He studied music in Leipzig but
dropped out of university at the age of
20. He got a job as a concert master in
Wurzburg and married a woman named
Minna. His first great work was an
opera entitled 'The Flying Dutchman'.
In 1864 he moved to Munich under the
patronage of the King of Bavaria. He
died of a heart attack in Venice in 1883.

2   Your partner will ask you questions about Wagner. Answer each question without
giving any further information. You may prompt questions like this:

You haven't asked me about . . .

When your partner has finished, he/she will try to repeat the information. Correct
errors like this:

No, actually . . .

3   Now it's your turn to ask questions.
Your partner has similar information about Salvador Dali.
Get this information by asking questions.
Try to remember what your partner tells you. You may write short notes if you wish.
When you've found out all you can, try to repeat it all.

20 Conversations

Don't look at your partner's book.

1   Your partner will ask you to talk about certain topics. Be talkative.

2   Get your partner to tell you all about:

his/her family
a recent problem
his/her most unpleasant memory
a recent change in his/her life

something he/she bought recently
a trip he/she is planning to make
the last party he/she went to
the last book he/she read

Find out as much as you can about each topic and try to keep your partner talking.
When you have finished, write brief notes about your partner's answers.

Useful language

Tell me about . . .
I'd like to hear all about . . .
I'd like to know a bit more about . . .

21 Newspaper Survey

Don't look at your partner's book.

1   Your partner is conducting a survey. Answer his/her questions helpfully.
2   You are conducting a survey too. Interview your partner to complete this questionnaire.

Begin like this:

Excuse me. I'm doing a survey on newspapers. Can I ask you some questions?

End like this: I see. Thank you very much.

---

number of newspapers read per day or ☐ per week: ☐   usual reading place:

average time spent per newspaper: ☐   usual reading time:

favourite newspaper:

reasons for preference:

cost of newspaper: opinion of cost: expensive / inexpensive

---

	like	dislike	indifferent	why?
international news	☐	☐	☐	
local news	☐	☐	☐	
business news	☐	☐	☐	
sports news	☐	☐	☐	
editorials	☐	☐	☐	
readers' letters	☐	☐	☐	
horoscope	☐	☐	☐	
TV and radio	☐	☐	☐	
cultural events	☐	☐	☐	
classified ads.	☐	☐	☐	

reasons for reading newspapers: information/amusement/other

Opinions: yes   no

Newspapers should be politically independent   ☐   ☐

Newspapers should be subsidised by advertising   ☐   ☐

opinion of your newspaper: satisfactory ☐   unsatisfactory ☐

---

further comments:

22 Crossword puzzle 1

Don't look at your partner's book.

You and your partner each have some of the answers to a crossword puzzle. You have no clues, however. Try to complete the puzzle by asking each other for clues,

E.g. What's seven across? It means . . . What's three down? It's . . .

You may use a bilingual dictionary to check the meaning of a word shown on your part of the crossword puzzle but don't look for definitions in a dictionary.

Don't tell your partner any of the words he/she needs, only clues.

Don't ask for confirmation of your guesses until you have completed the puzzle.

Useful language

Can you give me another clue?
Can you tell me your clue for seven across again?
Shall I give you another clue?

23 The Statue of Liberty

Don't look at your partner's book.

1   Read this article about the Statue of Liberty carefully.

2   Now answer your partner's questions. Don't give further information.

3   Your partner will check his/her information. Answer like this:

Yes, that's right.
No, actually . . .

In 1851, Frederick-Auguste Bartholdi watched a girl with a torch leap over a barricade and die during a revolution in Paris. The scene impressed him so much that he was inspired to build a great statue as a symbol of freedom. His model was a girl named Jeanne de Puysieux whom he met in a café. The statue was built in Paris and presented to the United States as a tribute to American democracy. It was taken by ship to New York and erected on Bedloe's Island, where it was unveiled on October 28 1886 by President Cleveland. Known throughout the world as the Statue of Liberty, it is impressive even today. Made of iron and copper weighing over 200 tons, it rises to a height of 305 feet.

B

24 Himeji Castle

Don't look at your partner's book.

1   Look at the picture carefully for a minute.

Where do you think this building is?
Have you ever seen it? Would you like to? What do you think of it?

2   Fill in the blanks in the following article about Himeji Castle by asking your partner questions.

Himeji Castle is one of the finest in _____. Although it was designed from the

viewpoint of _____, it is so graceful that it is called the '_____

_____'. The main keep is _____ stories high, and from the top the _____

_____ can be seen. In addition to high walls made of _____,

there used to be _____ moats, although only one still remains. The original

castle was built in the _____th Century; the present building, however, was

constructed in 16____ by the son-in-law of _____ _____. It took over

_____ years to build the castle, which stands on a small _____ overlooking

the _____ _____.

3   Now check your information like this:

Himeji Castle is in . . . , isn't it?

It was . . . , wasn't it?

25 Spot the differences

Don't look at your partner's book.

Your partner will describe a picture similar to yours.

1 Try to find ten or more differences between his/her picture and yours. Ask any questions you wish but don't look at your partner's picture. Make notes of each difference.

2 Have you found ten or more differences? Now try to describe your partner's picture without looking at it.

26 Idioms, proverbs and quotes

Try to work out with your partner what the following idioms, proverbs and quotes mean. You may look up individual words in a dictionary but try to explain your interpretations using words you already know. When you and your partner have agreed on a definition, write it down.

1 **Idioms**

a) take for a ride

E.g. He said, 'Look at these silver spoons I bought for only five pounds'. I examined them and said, 'I'm afraid you've been taken for a ride. They're made of stainless steel, not silver'.

b) the tip of the iceberg

E.g. The police have caught a few children using dangerous drugs. I'm afraid this is just the tip of the iceberg.

c) kill two birds with one stone
E.g. Our old house was too small and too far from the station so we decided to kill two birds with one stone and buy a bigger house near the station.

2   **Proverbs**

a) Make hay while the sun shines.

b) Don't count your chickens before they're hatched.

c) No news is good news.

3   **Quotes**

a) To impatient drivers – 'It's better to arrive late in this world than early in the next.'

b) 'Death is the great equaliser.'

c) Confucius – 'Better a diamond with a flaw than a pebble without one.'

Useful language

What do you think . . . means?

It ${could \atop might}$ mean . . .

I ${guess \atop suppose}$ it means . . .

Let me give an example.

27 Tourist information 1

Choose a partner who does not come from the same town as you.

You are going to visit your partner's home town. Find out what you need to know about:

how to get there from here
where to stay
what to see
where to eat

where to shop
what to buy (typical souvenirs)
how to get around
what to do in the evenings   etc.

Then ask a bit about the town itself, e.g.

geographical location
historical background

size and population
main industries   etc.

Finally, ask your partner to help you make a plan:

when to go
how to get there

how long to stay
what to do each day   etc.

Useful language

Could you tell me . . .?
Can you recommend . . .?

. . . should I . . .?
. . . do you suggest I . . .?

28 Tourist information 2

Answer your partner's questions about your country. Your partner knows, or will pretend to know, little about your country. Be as helpful as you can.

29 Discussion

Can you think of any good ways to:

get rich quickly?
learn to speak English fluently?
live to the age of 100?
find your future husband or wife?
cut the number of traffic accidents?
protect your home from thieves?
spend 10 dollars?
spend 10 thousand dollars?
become famous?
spend your life after retirement?

Discuss each question with your partner and try to choose the best answer.

Useful language

One way to . . . is to . . .
A better way is to . . .
What do you think?

I agree.
I disagree.
In my opinion, the best way is . . .

30 Resort island

You and your partner have bought a small island and want to develop it as a tourist resort in order to attract a lot of visitors. On the next page is your publicity brochure.

Discuss the details with your partner and then fill in the blanks together.

Next, discuss the best location for the amenities you have chosen (hotels, restaurants, sports facilities, etc.) and mark these on your map. Decide how much to charge for transport, entertainment, etc.

Finally, discuss how to publicise your resort and attract visitors in all seasons.

Useful language

What shall we . . .?
How about . . .?
Why don't we . . .
Let's . . .
I think we should . . .

That's a great idea.
I don't think that'd be a good idea.
I'd rather . . .
I think I'd prefer to . . .
Okay.

B

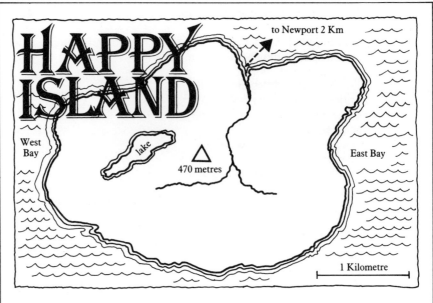

Come to Happy Island. There's fun for everybody!

For children, there's _____ and _____.

For adults, we have _____, _____ and _____.

Do you like sports? You can _____, _____ and _____ in summer.

You can _____ in winter; and you can _____ all year round.

We have accommodation to suit every budget. Stay in _____,

_____ or _____.

Our restaurants cater for all tastes. Eat _____ at the

or _____ at the _____.

You'll love travelling by _____ or _____ around the island.
(Sorry, no cars!)

Why not book your Happy Island holiday now?

Newport to Happy Island by _____ takes _____ minutes

and costs _____.

Admission fee is _____.

31 Treasure Island

Don't look at your partner's book.

You and your partner are going to look for treasure on an island. You each have a map with a different part of the route shown.

a) Explain to your partner the part of the route which you have, starting with the approach by sea to the only safe landing place, and giving appropriate warnings of danger as indicated by the symbols explained on the key.

b) Draw on your map the part of the route explained by your partner.

c) Discuss the best way to cross each river and the best route from the first bridge to the second.

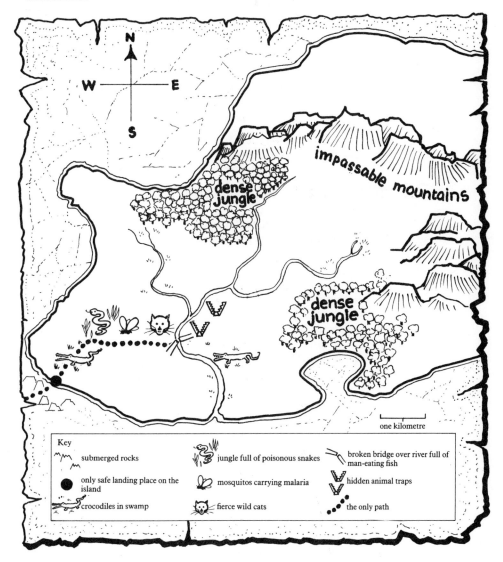

Useful language

Go south for about 200 metres.
Look out for tigers.
We'll have to make sure we (don't) . . .

32 The Grand Hotel

Don't look at your partner's book.

You would like to stay at the Grand Hotel.

1   Telephone the hotel and find out:

the location
the size
the number of rooms with bath or shower
whether each room has a television/telephone/heater
the amenities available within the hotel grounds (e.g. bar etc.)
the amenities in the vicinity (you like sports)
the distance from a) the nearest station b) the beach
the charge for a single room with bath.

2   Then make a reservation (if possible with a view of the sea).

Begin like this:

Good morning. I'm thinking of staying at your hotel. Could you give me a little information?
I'd like to know . . .   Could you tell me . . .

Make a reservation like this:
I'd like to make a reservation for . . . nights from . . .

33 Homestay programme

You organise homestay/study programmes in the U.K. This year you have arranged the following summer programme:

> Stay with an English family in beautiful Bournemouth (on the south coast of England) and learn English at the Anglo Academy for 3 hours each morning from Monday to Friday. Accommodation with breakfast and evening meal will be provided in a convenient location. You will have your own room and door key. At school, you will study practical English in small classes (maximum 10 students) and make friends from all over the world. At the end of the course, you will receive a certificate of graduation (there are no exams!) Afternoons and evenings will be free for swimming, shopping, sightseeing, etc. but weekend excursions to local places of interest (museums, theatres, etc.) are planned.
>
> The total charge, including tuition, accommodation and meals for 1 month is 320 pounds.
>
> Transportation to and from Bournemouth is not included.

Someone is going to telephone for information about the programme. Answer his/her questions and try to persuade him/her to join.

Begin like this: Good morning. Homestay International.

Useful language
This programme is just right for you.
I'm sure you'll enjoy it.
The (classes) are very (interesting).

34 Topics

Don't look at your partner's book.

1   Get your partner to talk for two minutes on each of these topics.

penguins   sand   winter
       dragons   toothache

If your partner remains silent for more than ten seconds during the talk, impose a penalty of one minute extra speaking time.

Start like this: Tell me what you know about . . .

2   Your partner will ask you to talk for two minutes on certain other topics. Once you start, you must keep talking. If you remain silent for more than ten seconds during the talk, you will have to talk for an extra minute as a penalty.

If you need time to think, use the following hesitation techniques.

Useful language

Hesitation: Penguins? er . . . mmm . . . Well . . .
               Let me see.
               How shall I put it?
               and . . . also . . . so . . .

Rephrasing: I mean . . .
               What I want to say is . . .
               Let me put it another way.

35 Explanations

Don't look at your partner's book.

1   Get your partner to explain the following. Insist on a clear explanation, even if you already understand. Don't correct your partner even if you know he/she is wrong.

a) the meaning of: bridge cigarette dream farm

b) the difference between 'boil' and 'fry'

c) the geographical features of your partner's country (mountains, lakes, islands, population centres, etc.)

d) how to play a certain card or board game

e) how to make an omelette or other simple meal

Useful language

Could you tell me what . . . means?

Can you explain . . .?

Pardon? Sorry? I'm afraid I don't understand
                        didn't follow you.

Would you mind explaining that again?
                             another way?

Sorry but I still don't understand . . .

I see. You mean . . .?

2   Your partner will ask you to explain some things too. Do your best. Use your imagination if necessary. You must give an explanation but it doesn't matter if you are wrong. Do not use a dictionary. Try to explain using words you already know.

Useful language

Pardon? Sorry?

Could you spell that?

I $\frac{think}{believe}$ it means . . .

I'm not sure but I $\frac{think}{suppose}$ . . .

I don't know $\frac{exactly}{much}$ about . . . but I $\frac{think}{guess}$ . . .

36 The Lotus Excel

Don't look at your partner's book.

You are thinking of buying a Lotus Excel sports car.
Find out from the salesman:

the price   the top speed
the average fuel consumption   the cruising range
the engine capacity   the number of seats
the luggage space   the number of gears

if the price includes:

power steering   stereo equipment
air conditioning   alloy wheels
if you may have a test drive

Begin like this: I'm thinking of buying . . . Can you tell me a bit about it?

37 House for sale

You are moving to another town and want to sell your house. You advertised it in yesterday's newspaper. Someone interested in buying it is going to phone you. Answer his/her inquiries and arrange for him/her to view the house.

If you don't have a house, use your imagination or talk about a relative's or friend's house instead.

38 Tall story 1

Don't look at your partner's book.

He/she is going to tell you about an experience he/she has just had. Be sceptical. Ask a lot of questions and try to prove that he/she is making the story up.

Useful language

You must be joking.
Are you really serious?
You can't expect me to believe that.

39 Tall story 2

You've just seen this scene.
Tell your partner all about it.
Answer his/her questions precisely because he/she is very sceptical and might not believe you.

Begin like this: You probably won't believe me but . . .

40 Opinions 1

Discuss with your partner and decide together:

a) the most useful possession you both have

b) the best film you've both seen

c) the most unusual thing you've both seen

d) the best book you've both read

e) the worst habit you both have

f) the most interesting place you've both visited

g) the best TV programme you both watch

h) the most unpleasant experience you've both had

E.g.
A What's your most useful possession?
B Let me see. My bicyle, I suppose.
A Oh. I haven't got a bicycle.
   I think my most useful possession is my calculator.
   Have you got a calculator?
B Yes, but I don't think it's very useful. How about . . .?

Useful language

Have you got . . .?	I think . . .	I agree/disagree.
Have you ever . . .?	I suppose . . .	Surely . . . is more . . .

B

41 Sketches

Don't let your partner see your book.

1   Your partner will tell you how to draw his/her picture. Draw it in the space on the right of your page next to your picture. Try to guess what it is.

2   Tell your partner how to draw your picture. Don't say what it is – let **him/her** guess.

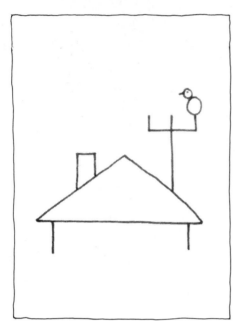

your picture

your partner's picture

Useful language

Draw a horizontal line from $\begin{matrix}\text{vertical}\\\text{diagonal}\end{matrix}$ ~~~ $\begin{matrix}\text{top left}\\\text{bottom right}\end{matrix}$ to . . .

This line is $\begin{matrix}\text{half}\\\text{twice}\end{matrix}$ as long as . . .

This line is the same length as . . .

Draw a $\begin{matrix}\text{large}\\\text{small}\end{matrix}$ $\begin{matrix}\text{square}\\\text{circle}\\\text{triangle}\\\text{rectangle}\end{matrix}$ $\begin{matrix}\text{above}\\\text{below}\end{matrix}$ . . .

From the $\begin{matrix}\text{middle}\\\text{end}\end{matrix}$ of this line, . . .

Sorry but I didn't understand. Could you say that again?
I see. The vertical line goes from . . . to . . .
How long is this line? How big is the circle?

42 News

1   You have just read this morning's 'Herald'.
These were the headlines:

    Hijack   Soccer Fans Riot   Treasure Found

    Imagine the details.

    Your partner is going to ask you questions about each report. Answer every question.

2   Your partner has just read a different newspaper, 'The Times'. Find out what the
main news was in that newspaper. Ask questions to get as many details as you can.

    Begin like this: Anything interesting in 'The Times' today?

43 Scandal

1   Someone saw you doing some very strange things yesterday and told your partner
about it. Explain your behaviour to your partner's satisfaction.

    Useful language

    Well actually it's rather embarrassing. / hard to explain. You see, . . .

2   Your partner has also been seen behaving strangely.
According to a reliable witness, he/she was:

    getting into a police car with a saucepan on his/her head at 8 a.m.

    pushing a wheelbarrow full of false teeth at 3 p.m.

    climbing a tree, wearing pyjamas at midnight.

    Demand a proper explanation. Find out as much as you can about the surrounding
circumstances and how the incidents are related.

    Useful language

    A friend of mine saw you . . .ing . . . at . . . o'clock.

    What on earth were you up to? / were you doing that for? / was going on?

B

44 Countries

Don't look at your partner's book.

	ALBANIA	ECUADOR	ICELAND	YOUR PARTNER'S COUNTRY
Location	S.E. Europe			
Population	3 million			
Language	Albanian			
Religion	atheist			
Capital city	Tirane			
Highest mountain	Tomor 2700 metres			
Biggest export	chromium			
Life expectancy	72 years			
Political system	communist republic			

1   Working by yourself, fill in as many spaces as you can in the chart. You have only five minutes to do this.

2   Working with a partner,
    a) Confirm what you've written in the second column, e.g. Ecuador's in . . . , isn't it?

Find out what you don't know, e.g. What religion do most . . .?

b) Answer your partner's questions about Albania.

c) Compare your ideas about Iceland like this:

I think . . .   So do I./Do you? I think . . .
Do you know . . .?   I'm not sure but I think . . .
                                 No. I'm afraid I have no idea.

d) Confirm what you have written about your partner's country and find out what you don't know.

e) Answer your partner's questions about your country.

3   Listen carefully. Your teacher will tell you all you need to know about Iceland. Fill in the spaces with the correct data. What did you find most surprising?

4   Discuss with your partner which of the countries you have just talked about you would most or least like to live in. Why?

45 Stories 1

Don't look at your partner's book.

1 You have a diamond. How you got it is shown below. Tell your partner the story, making it seem as interesting as you can. Use your imagination to fill in the details.

2 Your partner has a gold coin. Find out exactly how he/she got it. Ask a lot of questions to get the whole story.

46 Stories 2

Don't look at your partner's book.

Two separate stories have got mixed up. You have some sentences from each story. Your partner has the other sentences. Work out the two complete stories with your partner without looking at each other's sentences.

When they looked back, the boat had disappeared.

He took out his hammer and started to break the bridge.

The magician and the parrot jumped into a lifeboat and escaped.

A magician got a job on a big ship.

He came to a low bridge.

He entertained the passengers with numerous tricks.

'That wouldn't be any use,' said the old man. 'It's my donkey's ears that are too long, not his legs!'

The parrot wasn't impressed with the act because it saw the same tricks every night.

'It's too low. My donkey can't go under it,' said the old man.

Useful language

What do you think the first sentence is?
I think I've got a sentence which comes before that.
Can you tell me your second sentence again?
Sorry, can you say that again?

47 Nepal

Don't look at your partner's book.

1 Think about the following questions for a minute.

Have you ever been to Nepal? Would you like to go? What kind of place do you think it is? What do you know about it? In what ways does it differ from your own country?

2 Fill in the blanks in the following article by asking your partner questions.

Nepal is a small country located between _____ and _____. It extends

_____ miles from east to west and _____ miles from north to south and has a total

area of _____ square miles. It consists of _____ distinct regions: the _____,

_____ the _____ _____ and the _____

_____. The rainy season lasts from _____ to _____ and the

average rainfall is _____ inches per year. The climate is temperate in the mountains

and _____ in the plains, with a maximum temperature of ____F and a

minimum temperature of ____F.

Nepal has _____ million people, most of whom belong to the _____

or _____ racial groups and to one or other of the two main religions, _____

and _____. Most Nepalis are engaged in the production of _____,

their main food, or in _____, which is the country's principal source of

foreign currency. Nepal's political system may be described as a _____

_____. The present ruler's name is _____ _____.

48 New Zealand

1 Read this article about New Zealand. You may use a dictionary if you wish.

2 Answer your partner's questions about New Zealand.

New Zealand consists of two large islands (North and South Islands) and two small ones and has a total land area of about 100,000 square miles. It is located in the South Pacific Ocean about 1200 miles east of Australia. It used to be a British colony but gained full independence in 1947. Most of its 3.2 million population are descendants of British settlers but there are several thousand Maoris (the native people). The economy is based on agriculture, with wool, meat and dairy products accounting for nearly 80% of all exports.

South Island is very mountainous, with 15 peaks over 10,000 feet high. The highest, Mount Cook, is named after the British sea captain who first claimed the islands for Britain. On a clear day, South Island can be seen from North Island across the Cook Strait, a distance of 16 miles. The largest towns are Auckland and Wellington, the capital, both on North Island.

49 Opinions 2

Discuss with your partner and decide together what is:

a) the most significant event of the 20th century so far

b) the greatest invention or discovery waiting to be made

c) the biggest danger facing the world today

d) the nation which has contributed most to human development

e) the most difficult aspect of English for foreign students

f) the most important quality needed by a good teacher

Useful language

As I see it, . . .
If you ask me, . . .
I suppose . . .

Really? But don't you think . . .?
Yes, that's just what I think.

50 Crossword puzzle 2

Don't look at your partner's book.

You and your partner each have some of the answers to this crossword puzzle. However, you have no clues. Try to complete the puzzle by asking each other for clues, not words.

E.g. What's 7 across? What's 1 down?

You may use a bilingual dictionary to check the meaning of a word shown on your part of the crossword puzzle but don't look for definitions in a dictionary.

Don't tell your partner any of the words he/she needs, only clues.

Don't ask for confirmation of your guesses.

Two words are missing. Try to guess these and make up appropriate clues.

51 Lock

Don't look at your partner's book.

Find out from your partner what a canal lock is used for and how it works. Try to draw a diagram.

Useful language

Can you tell me . . .?
Sorry but I don't understand.

Would you mind explaining that again?
I see.

B

52 Water lift

Explain to your partner how a water lift works without showing the diagram.

Useful language

It is used for . . .   Are you with me?
It consists of . . .   OK?
When someone wants to go up, down, . . .   You see?

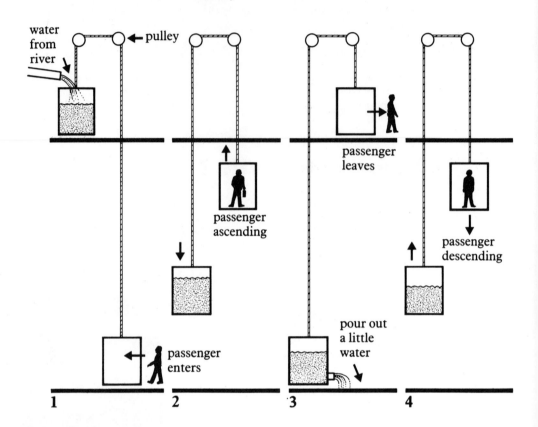

53 Job interview 1

Don't look at your partner's book.

You are applying for a job with a travel agency. The manager is going to interview you. Answer each question truthfully. When he/she has no more questions, try to find out the following information about the job:

duties   wages
working hours   holidays with pay
pension   fringe benefits
if accommodation provided

Begin like this: Good morning. My name's . . .

Ask about the job like this: May I ask a few questions about the job? I'd like to know . . . Could you tell me?

End like this: It was nice meeting you. I look forward to hearing from you soon. Goodbye.

54 Job interview 2

1   You run a language school in London. Someone is applying for a job in your school as a teacher of his/her native language.
    Interview him/her and fill out this form.

Details of applicant

NAME

ADDRESS

TEL. NO.

DATE OF BIRTH

AGE

PLACE OF BIRTH

NATIONALITY

PRESENT OCCUPATION

MARITAL STATUS

ANY CHILDREN

DETAILS OF PREVIOUS EMPLOYMENT

EDUCATIONAL BACKGROUND (SECONDARY SCHOOL AND COLLEGE)

QUALIFICATIONS

PREVIOUS TEACHING EXPERIENCE

REASONS FOR APPLYING FOR A JOB AT THIS SCHOOL

---

2   Ask the applicant if he/she has any questions.
    Here are some details about the job:

The teacher will work from 4 to 9 p.m. Monday to Saturday teaching his/her native language to Britons aged 18–40. He/she will be paid 120 pounds per week and will receive 8 days paid holiday per year, to be taken between October and March. Commutation expenses will be paid but there will be no private pension. The contract will last for one year.

Begin like this: Pleased to meet you, . . . I'd like to start by asking you a few questions, if I may.

End like this: Well I think that's all. We'll inform you of our decision in a few days. Thank you for coming.

55 A deliberate mistake

Don't look at your partner's book.

You and your partner each have a picture.

In each picture the artist has made a deliberate mistake, e.g. something is missing or is in the wrong place.

Find out what is wrong with your partner's picture by asking questions.

Answer your partner's questions about your picture but do not help him/her to guess the mistake.

56 Contest

Work with a partner. Try to finish before the other students.

1   Work out together what these abbreviations stand for:

P T O   R I P   G M T   V I P   PhD   o n o   c/o   Ltd

Ave   Sq

2   Complete these similes. If you don't know the standard expression, use your imagination.

as weak as a *kitten*	as deaf as	to run like
as old as	as fit as	to eat like
as mad as	to sing like *a bird*	to smoke like
as thin as	to swim like	to sleep like

3   Write down:

6 words whose plural form doesn't end in s	3 occupations dealing with animals
5 things you can do with an umbrella	2 kinds of birds
4 kinds of catastrophe	1 word meaning 'cannot be anticipated'

57 Deductions

Don't look at your partner's book.

Try to solve this puzzle with your partner by exchanging information and deductions. Do not write down your partner's sentences. You may only write data in the space beneath each house.

There are five houses in Mill Lane. Each is a different colour and is occupied by one person. Each person has a different job and uses a different vehicle.

Work out the following details about each person:

his/her name   the colour of his/her house
his/her occupation   the vehicle he/she uses
where he/she lives

Clues

Miss Jones lives in a blue house.
There is a Rolls Royce in the garage of the red house.
Mr Harris lives next door to a banker.
The waitress has a bicycle.
Mr Clark is a dentist.
There is a motorbike outside the yellow house.
The hairdresser has a scooter.
One of the houses is white.

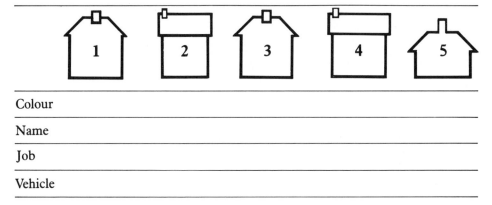

Colour					
Name					
Job					
Vehicle					

58 Impressions

Find out what your partner thought of your English course.

Talk about:

the curriculum   the materials used
the teachers   the other students
the cost   the classroom facilities
the length of the course   your partner's progress

Agree or disagree with your partner's comments and talk about your own impressions.

Useful language

What do you think of . . .?   I thought so too.
How did you find . . .?   Oh, I wouldn't say that.
I thought it was quite/very . . .   Why do you think so?
I found it quite/very . . .